AF251445

OSPREYS

OSPREYS

by DOROTHY HINSHAW PATENT

photographs by WILLIAM MUÑOZ

CLARION BOOKS · NEW YORK

ACKNOWLEDGMENTS
The author and photographer wish to thank Maggie Anderson, Steve and Eileen Beck,
Pat Gonzales, Cal Henry, and Pacific Power and Light of Kalispell, Montana.

Clarion Books
a Houghton Mifflin Company imprint
215 Park Avenue South, New York, NY 10003
Text copyright © 1993 by Dorothy Hinshaw Patent
Photographs copyright © 1993 by William Muñoz

Printed in Singapore.
Book design by Carol Goldenberg.

Library of Congress Cataloging-in-Publication Data
Patent, Dorothy Hinshaw.
Ospreys / by Dorothy Hinshaw Patent ; photographs by
William Muñoz.
p.   cm.
Includes bibliographical references (p. 59) and index.
Summary: Describes the physical characteristics and
habits of ospreys, or fish hawks, as well as threats to their
survival and efforts to protect them.
ISBN 0-395-63391-5
1. Ospreys—Juvenile literature. [1. Ospreys.] I.
Muñoz, William, ill. II. Title.
QL696.F36P38   1993
598'.917—dc20   92-30103
                                              CIP
                                              AC

TWP 10 9 8 7 6 5 4 3 2 1

*To all those helping bring back the osprey,
especially in the lower Flathead Valley.*

Contents

1

OSPREYS

I t's hard not to know when ospreys (called *Pandion haliaetus* by scientists) are around. Their nests are huge, weigh up to half a ton (4500 kilograms), and crown the tops of dead trees, power poles, and nesting platforms near water. Only the nests of bald eagles rival those of ospreys. These eye-catching birds fly over water in search of fish, their white breasts reflecting the light, their whistlelike calls attracting the ear.

RECOGNIZING THE OSPREY

The osprey is a unique bird. While it is related to hawks and eagles, scientists place it in its own special group. The underside of the osprey's body is white or mottled, while the feathers on the back are very dark brown. Some ospreys have a dark band across the breast. Their heads are white, with black marks across the cheeks and on the crown. Their bright yellow eyes

Ospreys are generally seen near water.

are intense. Although there are differences among ospreys from around the world, their appearance is remarkably similar everywhere.

Male ospreys weigh from 2½ pounds (1.1 kilograms) to 3½ pounds (1.6 kilograms), while females are heavier, up to 4½ pounds (almost 2 kilograms). Ospreys have a wingspan as wide as 6 feet (1.8 meters), the size of a small eagle, but their wings are narrower than those of eagles.

When ospreys fly, their wings are usually partially bent into a V shape.

Ospreys in flight can be recognized by their slightly V-shaped wings with black markings just beyond the bend of the V. Unlike hawks and eagles with wider wings, ospreys rarely soar with the wings held in place; they are more likely to fly actively. When they are hunting, ospreys often hover over the water fluttering their wings.

You may first know an osprey is near by hearing its guard call, a slow, gentle whistle repeated several times as the pitch

A female osprey gives a guard call.

falls. The call is reminiscent of a whistling teakettle taken off the burner. The guard call is the osprey's way of responding to another osprey nearing its nest. Ospreys also make high-pitched whistles or squeals when they feel threatened and deeper rasping notes when someone approaches too close to the nest.

Ospreys are relatively long-lived birds. They can survive into their twenties and still breed.

HUNTING FOR FISH

Another name for the osprey is fish hawk, and for good reason. Ninety-nine percent of the osprey's diet consists of live fish, caught in spectacular dives of 15 to 215 feet (5 to 70 meters). Ospreys are almost always found near the water, especially where it is shallow and calm. They aren't particular—they eat whatever fish are abundant and easy to catch. They can reach about three feet (a meter) into the water when they dive, so they can only capture fish relatively close to the surface. Choppy water makes it difficult for the birds to spot their prey.

A hunting fish hawk flies slowly over the water, searching for fish near the surface. Now and then it hovers, fluttering its wings in place, as it spies a likely target. When it zeroes in on its

An osprey flies high over the water, looking for fish.

After spotting possible prey, the bird dives down. When it hits the water, its talons fasten tightly onto the fish.

prey, the bird tucks its wings into V's above its back and dives steeply down. Its head and feet are stretched out in front and its fanned-out tail makes small adjustments to keep the bird on course as it plummets downward, its gaze riveted on its target. The bird hits the water with a big splash and may disappear in the spray for a moment, emerging with a struggling fish gripped firmly in its sharp, curved talons.

Ospreys are very powerful, capable of rising out of the water carrying fish weighing 30 percent of their body weight. After striking a fish, the bird may pause a moment on the water's surface, adjusting its grip on the struggling prey. Then it reaches up and back with its long, strong wings, sweeping them down-

Using its strong wings, the osprey pulls out of the water. Then it shakes itself dry before flying away to feed.

ward and forward, pulling itself up, dinner firmly grasped in its talons. Once airborne, the bird may shake itself to get rid of any excess water, then fly up and away, carrying the fish headfirst, which reduces air resistance. The osprey lands on a nearby perch and holds the fish tightly until it quits struggling. Then the bird begins to eat the fish, starting at the head.

The fish hawk is well adapted to its way of life. Its long legs have short, dense feathers on their upper parts and are bare from the knees down, allowing the bird to plunge into the water with little resistance. Its long toes are of equal length and are covered on their lower surfaces by small rough spines, so the bird can grip slippery fish securely. Its claws are as long as

The osprey's strong claws grip the fish firmly.

its toes and are strongly curved and sharply pointed so they can penetrate easily. The claws grasp lightning-fast, clutching on to a fish in 1/50 of a second. An osprey can rotate its outer toes, so it can grab a fish with two toes in front and two behind. The dense, short, oily feathers on its body repel water so that the bird doesn't become waterlogged when it plunges after its prey. Its hooked beak has a sharp tip for tearing flesh.

An osprey doesn't need to work hard to feed itself. One to three fish is all it takes to fuel its body for a day. When food is abundant, a skilled bird can catch what it needs in only a half-hour of fishing.

WORLD TRAVELER

The osprey is one of the most familiar birds in the world because of its wide distribution along shorelines and riverbeds. Ospreys nest on four continents—North America, Europe,

Ospreys nest along coastlines (here at Cape Romain National Wildlife Refuge in South Carolina) as well as near rivers and shallow lakes.

Asia, and Australia. Most ospreys migrate to the tropics for the winter. Only those living around Baja California, in Florida, in parts of the Caribbean and Mediterranean, and in the Middle East live in the same area year round.

Migration begins in late summer, after the young birds have left the nest and learned how to take care of themselves. Some birds travel a long distance. Ospreys that nest in Finland and Sweden migrate all the way south to West Africa, a distance of 2800 to 3900 miles (4500 to 6000 kilometers). Birds nesting in North America spend the winter in Central and South America. The birds seem to stick to coastlines when possible. Along the Atlantic coast of North America, hundreds of ospreys may pass over a particular spot the same day.

Ospreys arrive at their winter homes by late November. The adult birds stay until late February or early March, then head back to their nesting areas. Only young birds hatched the previous year remain on the wintering grounds until the next spring, when they join their elders on the flight north. Even though most of them fly to the breeding grounds at the age of two, ospreys don't pair up and have families until they are at least three years old.

Ospreys' powerful wings can carry them long distances in migration.

2

OSPREYS AT HOME

Altogether, there are about eight thousand breeding pairs of ospreys in North America. They nest throughout Florida and all the way up the east coast to north of the island of Newfoundland in Canada. Traveling westward, nesting ospreys are found in a broad band across southern Canada into Alaska, dipping downward into the United States in Maine, around the Great Lakes, and in the Rocky Mountains and Pacific Northwest. On the west coast, ospreys don't breed from south of San Francisco Bay almost to Baja California, probably because those coastal waters are too rough.

STARTING A HOME

Ospreys begin nesting in early springtime, arriving at their breeding grounds about the time when the ice breaks up and fish begin to move into shallow waters. Older birds usually

An osprey repairing an old nest.

arrive first, with mated pairs almost always reusing their nest from the previous year. Ospreys become very attached to their nesting site. Even when their old nest is damaged beyond repair during the winter, the birds stay nearby, building a new nest no farther than 5 miles (8 kilometers) away from the old one.

Birds without mates must pair up after arriving in the breeding area. It is the male's job to attract the female. He does so by performing a "sky dance," flying overhead with dramatic dips and dives, rhythmically calling "eeeet-eeeet-eeeet." Most often,

Male ospreys call during their courtship sky dance.

hc carries a fresh fish or a choice piece of nesting material in his talons as he displays himself.

Where food and nest sites are abundant, ospreys may nest very close together. While the birds defend their nests against other ospreys, they share the feeding grounds. In areas like the east coast of the United States, osprey nests may be as close together as 65 feet (20 meters). But at the northern extreme of the breeding range, there may be only one pair for miles around. Wherever they build their nests, ospreys need not fly more than 6½ miles (10 kilometers) to find food.

Ospreys often nest close together.

The male feeds his potential mate, who sits at the nest site and begs from him like a young chick. It is not clear whether the female is more influenced by the quality of the nest site or by the quantity of fish provided by her mate, but it is very important for her to choose a mate that can fish well. She and the chicks will depend on him completely for food until the young birds learn to fly.

A pair of ospreys at their nest.

24

While the chicks are growing, the male must work hard to get enough fish to feed his family. He needs to spend as much as a quarter of the day flying, looking for food. All that flying takes energy, so he needs to eat about twice as much as usual in addition to catching fish for his mate and chicks. Some males do a better job providing for their families than others. Even when there are plenty of fish, some males don't bring enough food, and some of their chicks die.

For a new pair, finding a nesting site can be difficult. If there are no abandoned nests nearby, they must find a new place that meets their needs. The site must be in the open so that the birds have a clear view in all directions, making it possible to fly to the nest without having to navigate through trees. It also must be wide enough and strong enough to support the enormous, heavy nest.

When protected by water, an osprey nest may be built lower than if on the shore.

Ospreys' nests aren't always high up. Open water provides an effective barrier to predators like raccoons and snakes, and the birds often build their nests on large buoys or channel markers. Islands are favorite sites as well, especially small ones likely to be free of predators.

The base of the nest is made with sticks. Ospreys are strong enough to grab a dead branch and break it off a tree trunk. When enough branches have been piled to provide a strong, stable foundation, the birds bring softer material, such as seaweed and grass, to line the nest. Both birds bring nesting material, but the female tends to stay at the nest and arrange the material while the male brings more. Old nests require some rebuilding each year. Winter damage is repaired and a fresh, soft lining added.

The osprey collects sticks for the base of the nest, and softer material to line the nest. At far right, an osprey arrives with nesting material.

An osprey's-eye view of eggs in the nest.

FAMILY LIFE

The birds mate often as the nest is being built. As egg-laying approaches, mating becomes even more frequent and the male guards his mate closely. The two to four eggs are usually laid ten to thirty days after the birds arrive, depending on whether they have already chosen mates and nest sites. Osprey eggs are mottled in color, with a creamy white to tan background marked with brown or reddish brown blotches. They are about the same size as chicken eggs.

The birds take turns incubating, with the female on the

28

Osprey eggs.

nest more often than the male. Each bird has a bare patch of skin on its breast that it snuggles up against the eggs, keeping them warm.

It takes five to six weeks for the eggs to hatch. The chick inside the egg has a special egg tooth at the tip of its upper beak that it uses to break through the shell. The chick is helpless and awkward at first, but gains strength fast. Its body is covered by soft tan down, and its eyes open within a few hours of hatching. From the beginning, the chick can take food from its mother's beak.

A parent feeds a chick (top). These osprey chicks (center) still have some down, but their other feathers are growing in fast. The chicks flatten themselves against the nest (bottom), their patterned feathers helping to camouflage them.

After the male bird brings a fish to the nest, the female pecks at it and tears off small pieces of meat to feed to the chicks. By the time the chicks are ten to twelve days old, they have grown a thick covering of black, woolly feathers. Their legs are grayish blue and their small, sharp claws are black. They are strong enough to fight over food if there isn't enough to eat. A larger chick may peck at a smaller one, preventing it from feeding. If this behavior continues, the weaker chick may not get enough to eat and may slowly starve. But if there is plenty to eat, the stronger chick lets its siblings feed after its own hunger is satisfied, and all of them may survive.

Given enough to eat, the young birds grow fast. By the time they are a month old, they have already reached 70 to 80 percent of their adult weight. By then, their feathers have grown in and they look like adult ospreys, although their coloring is more mottled. They flap their wings energetically, strengthening the muscles that will soon allow them to fly.

Two chicks almost ready to fly.

31

One tries his wings.

Bit by bit, the young birds get closer to flying. As they get stronger, they stand on the edge of the nest, facing into the wind and jumping up and down while beating their wings. At any moment, the wind can pick up a young bird and carry it away from the nest, forcing it to fly.

Being able to fly, however, is only the first step to independence for the young ospreys. They still depend on their parents for food. Learning to fish is a very individual matter. Some youngsters are able to catch fish only a few days after leaving the nest. But more often, it takes a couple of weeks before they are good enough hunters. It takes time before the young birds are as successful as adults at catching fish. For the first six months, they have about half the hunting success rate of their parents.

Leaving the nest, even to travel a short distance, is a big accomplishment.

Until they are able to feed themselves completely, the young ospreys continue to return to the nest and beg for food from their parents. Sometimes the chicks will visit other nests nearby and be fed there. It seems that ospreys are not able to recognize their own offspring and will feed any chick that begs at their nest.

By late August, all the osprey youngsters are on their own, and the birds begin their trip south, unless they live in a mild climate where fish are available year round. Some young birds may hang around their nests for a few days after their parents have departed, but most leave around the same time as the older birds.

Even after learning to fly, a young osprey is fed by its parents as it learns to fish for itself.

3

THREATS TO OSPREYS

As a species, ospreys are in good shape today, with about twenty-five to thirty thousand breeding pairs worldwide. However, ospreys are scarce in some areas where they were once common. For example, only a few ospreys nest in the Mediterranean. There, only scattered pairs breed on a few islands and on remote parts of the coast. Greece is one of the few countries in the world that doesn't protect this magnificent fish hunter, and shooting ospreys is a popular sport in that part of the world. Even where the law protects the birds, many may still be shot, as such laws are difficult to enforce.

Typical osprey habitat.

Ospreys are well able to defend their nests from intruders.

Natural Enemies

Like other large birds of prey, ospreys have few natural enemies. Not many creatures could win out over this predator's strong, sharp beak and talons. This is one reason it is safe for ospreys to nest in such conspicuous places. The only predators that can sometimes catch an adult osprey unawares are large owls that attack incubating females on the nest. Eggs and nestlings may sometimes be lost to hawks, eagles, or owls, but flying predators are not a major threat to osprey survival.

In North America, the greatest natural enemy of ospreys is the raccoon. This intelligent animal can climb trees and steal osprey eggs. When raccoons are abundant they can be a real threat to osprey survival. In one osprey colony in the United States, as many as half the nests were attacked by raccoons each year, until people stepped in and put metal guards on nest trees to foil the raccoons.

Bald eagles sometimes take over osprey nests.

This young great horned owl may grow up to feed on osprey chicks.

39

Old dead trees near the shore are prime osprey nesting places.

Many ospreys spend the winter along the Tempisque River in western Costa Rica. Photo by Dorothy H. Patent.

When osprey populations fall, we know there are serious problems with the environment. Fortunately, reduced numbers of ospreys are hard to miss, since their presence or absence is so obvious. This makes the osprey a conspicuous indicator of the ecological health of a region. Because it feeds at the top of the aquatic food chain, the osprey quickly falls victim to contaminants in water that collect in fish tissues or that kill the food it depends on. Since fish hawks require old trees for nesting, they can't survive where logging has stripped the shores of lakes and rivers. In such areas, even providing nest sites may not help ospreys if logging has led to erosion. When too much soil laid bare by logging is carried into waterways, fish reproduction can drop drastically, and ospreys are hard pressed to find enough to eat.

The current extensive logging of the tropical rain forests also threatens ospreys, along with the other North American birds that spend up to half their lives in the tropics. While ospreys don't nest in the tropics (except for a few in Asia), logging there leads to erosion and silting. The silt that clogs rivers also damages reefs and other coastal habitats that fish depend on for breeding.

CHEMICAL POLLUTION

When people working in laboratories develop chemicals for human uses, they are often unaware of the effects these substances can have on natural systems. While a variety of different manmade chemicals have caused ecological problems, the worst so far for ospreys and many other organisms have been the organochlorine compounds. When attached to molecules containing chains of carbon, chlorine can damage living systems. Insecticides such as DDT that take advantage of this characteristic were used in large amounts in the 1950s and 1960s. Dieldrin and aldrin are two related insecticides that can also harm birds and other living things.

When such chemicals are released into the environment, they are taken in by living things. Two traits make them especially dangerous: they collect in fatty tissues of the body and they last a long time. For these reasons, the concentration of organochlorine compounds increases with each step up the food chain. In an osprey's body, there can be a million times as much DDT as is in the water, and as much as a hundred times the amount that is in the fish it eats.

DDT is especially dangerous for ospreys. An osprey with a high concentration of DDT in its body may look and act normal. But when nesting time comes, there is trouble. The more DDT and DDE (a dangerous chemical produced by the bird from DDT) in the female's body, the thinner the shells of the eggs she lays. Eggs with thin shells can crack just from the weight of the incubating parent bird.

DDE can harm the egg in other ways too. Even when the shells don't crack, the developing chick inside may die either from poisoning or because the eggshell wasn't correctly formed. Shells have tiny holes in them that allow oxygen and

42

carbon dioxide to pass between the embryo and the air outside, and DDE interferes with the formation of these pores.

POPULATION CRASHES

During the 1960s, osprey populations in parts of the United States were dropping at an alarming rate, but no one knew the cause. At the same time, other large birds that fed on fish, such as bald eagles and pelicans, were also having trouble in some parts of the country. It wasn't long before scientists were able to pin the blame on DDT and other pesticides.

Other fish eaters besides ospreys, such as bald eagles, died in large numbers from DDT poisoning.

*By the mid-1980s, osprey nests were a common sight along roadsides
in Florida, where old power poles were set up for their use.*
Photo by Dorothy H. Patent.

Ospreys on the northeastern coast were hit the hardest. The breeding populations in a variety of locales were reduced by 50 to 90 percent. Some disappeared completely. Fortunately, when the pesticides were phased out during the late 1960s and early 1970s, ospreys recovered quite rapidly. By the late 1970s, the birds were again reproducing normally, and populations were growing.

THE OUTLOOK FOR OSPREYS

Altogether, ospreys have fared quite well in our crowded, contaminated world. But many threats to their survival remain. Pesticides like DDT are still used in the tropical countries where ospreys spend the winters. So far, the birds do not seem to have accumulated enough of these harmful chemicals to interfere with reproduction. But other manmade problems, such as mercury contamination and acid rain, which can harm the fish ospreys rely on, may cause trouble in the future.

Other threates continue too. People still shoot ospreys, especially when they feed on fish in ponds where fish are being raised for sale. Logging continues to reduce the number of nest sites and to decrease the food supply in many areas. As with other wild things, the increasing human population on the planet puts pressure both on the osprey's food supply and on the availability of places to nest.

4

HELPING THE OSPREY SURVIVE

In order to help species like the osprey survive, we need to understand and help to meet their needs. Ospreys are easier to help than many other wild species. For one thing, the shallow waters of the world still seem to produce enough fish for them to eat. For another, it is easy to supply nesting sites.

ENJOYING OSPREYS

Best of all, ospreys become used to the presence of humans and of civilization—noisy cars, trains, boats, and airplanes don't bother them when they choose to nest near people. As long as

Shallow marshes provide plenty of fish for ospreys.

Frogs and other birds, like this coot, share osprey habitat.

the disturbance is present at the time of nesting, the birds seem unruffled. However, ospreys that nest in a quiet place may be upset if it becomes noisy later. A pair of birds that chooses a nesting site in a quiet lakeside spot may be disturbed when people begin to use the campground next door. If noise bothers them, birds may abandon their nest and eggs.

Osprey watchers must be sensitive to the birds' needs. If you come across an osprey nest right along the road, chances are the birds won't be bothered if you watch them. But if you encounter one at a remote mountain lake, you should respect the birds' sensitivity and not venture too close. You should never climb a tree at or near an osprey nest, for your own sake as well as for the birds'. Ospreys are fierce defenders of their families and will dive at intruders, even striking them with their

Ospreys easily become accustomed to human activity.

powerful, sharp talons. It's best to keep a respectful distance between yourself and an osprey nest.

You aren't likely to disturb ospreys away from the nest. People enjoy watching these powerful birds make their spectacular dives. The best time to observe ospreys fishing is in early summer, after the eggs have hatched and the male bird has to catch enough fish for his chicks as well as for himself and his mate. Birds are most likely to fish early in the morning or late in the afternoon. If you can visit on a calm day just after a day or two of stormy weather, you may be able to see dive after dive after dive as the birds catch up on missed fishing time.

The beak and claws of an osprey could easily injure a person threatening the nest.

A nesting platform for ospreys has been placed on the top of this dead tree at Lee Metcalf National Wildlife Refuge in western Montana.

PROVIDING NEST SITES

In many areas, logging and residential development have reduced the number of good osprey nesting sites. Such places may have waters with plenty of fish for the birds to eat. But if there are no available places to build nests, the osprey population can't increase. Where there are plenty of nesting sites, ospreys can begin to breed when they are three years old. But where they must wait for older birds to die off, freeing nests, they may not start reproducing until the age of seven.

Before fur trappers decimated them, beavers provided perfect conditions for ospreys. A beaver dam backs up water that floods the land, killing trees. These trees can then serve as osprey nesting sites. The shallow beaver pond also makes an ideal fishing ground for the birds. In modern times, manmade dams accomplish much the same result. Trees die in flooded areas behind the dam, and ospreys can nest there.

But dead trees eventually rot away, and many ideal osprey habitats lack enough nest sites. Fortunately, providing nest sites

Old telephone poles make fine nesting sites.

for ospreys is quite easy. All it takes is a sturdy platform securely attached to the top of a dead tree or a pole. In some areas, ospreys have become pests by nesting on power poles. Their large nests can damage the wires. Or even worse, the birds can touch their wings to two wires at once, killing themselves and shorting out the power. Some companies solve this problem by putting up spiked poles where the birds can't nest. But others simply add an upper layer to the poles, safely above the wires, where the ospreys can nest in peace.

Even when a platform is added above power lines, material from osprey nests sometimes hangs over the lines and must be removed.

After the job is done, the osprey returns to the nest.

In shallow water, even simpler nesting devices work well. A tripod only a few feet tall, topped with a platform, makes a safe site that land-based predators can't reach.

REINTRODUCING OSPREYS

Because of pollution and habitat loss, ospreys have disappeared from some areas where they once lived. Now, if pollution is under control and nest sites are available, ospreys can move back. But ospreys tend to be homebodies, returning to the area where they were raised. Only when there are no available nest sites will the birds wander in search of new homes.

For example, ospreys were exterminated in Britain early in the twentieth century. Even though Scandinavian birds flew over Scotland on their migrations each year, it was only in the mid-1950s that ospreys began to breed there again.

54

It's easier for parents to raise young ospreys than for people to take on the job.

One way to speed osprey recolonization is to bring young birds to a new environment and raise them there. In recent years, scientists have used a method called hacking to return a variety of hawks and eagles as well as ospreys to their old haunts. In hacking, young birds are taken from captivity or from areas where the birds are abundant and brought to their new homes. They are placed in a protected place and fed by humans. When the birds are old enough to fly, they are gradually weaned away from being fed and encouraged to learn to hunt on their own. Hacked birds tend to return to the area where they were raised, eventually breeding there.

Hacking is expensive and takes a lot of work, so it is important to choose an area where ospreys once lived, one where the habitat is in good enough shape to support ospreys again. In those cases, this ingenious technique can help bring the magnificent osprey back to its old haunts, where it has always belonged.

BIBLIOGRAPHY

Edwards, Thomas C., Jr. "The ontogeny of diet selection in fledgling ospreys." *Ecology* 70 (1989): 881-896.

Johnsgard, Paul A. *Hawks, Eagles, and Falcons of North America.* Washington, D.C.: Smithsonian Institution Press, 1990.

Poole, Alan F. *Ospreys—A Natural and Unnatural History.* New York: Cambridge University Press, 1989.

Steidl, R. J.; and C. R. Griffin. "Growth and brood reduction of mid-Atlantic coast ospreys." *Auk* 108 (1991): 363-370.

Thibault, J. C.; and O. Patrimonio. "Some aspects of breeding success of the osprey *Pandion Haliaetus* in Corsica (Friace) West Mediterranean." *Bird Study* 38 (1991): 98-102.

INDEX

ABOUT THE AUTHOR AND PHOTOGRAPHER

DOROTHY HINSHAW PATENT holds a Ph.D. in zoology from the University of California at Berkeley. She has written more than seventy books for children and young adults on wildlife and wildlife management, most recently *Pelicans*. In 1987, Dr. Patent received the Eva L. Gordon Award for Children's Science Literature for the body of her work. She and her husband, Gregory Patent, have two grown sons. They live in Missoula, Montana.

WILLIAM MUÑOZ earned his B.A. degree in history from the University of Montana. He has collaborated with Dorothy Hinshaw Patent on many successful photo essays, including *Pelicans*. He lives with his wife, Sandy, and son, Sean, in St. Ignatius, Montana, where he divides his time between freelance photography and gardening.